BE YOUR OWN

MAP EXPERT

BARBARA TAYLOR

WITHDRAWN
University of
Reading Library

95 0249490 0

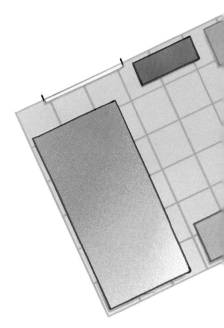

First published in 1993
by Simon & Schuster Young Books

Simon & Schuster Young Books
Campus 400
Maylands Avenue
Hemel Hempstead
Herts HP2 7EZ

© 1993 Simon & Schuster Young Books

Illustrator: Brett Breckon
Design: Celia Hart
Commissioning Editor: Debbie Fox
Copy Editor: Diana Russell

All rights reserved

Printed and bound in Belgium
by Proost International Book Production

A CIP catalogue record for this book is available
from the British Library

ISBN 0 7500 1326 5

CONTENTS

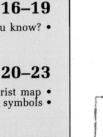

LL

UNIVERSITY
OF READING
BULMERSHE
LIBRARY

ACCESS No:
249490

CLASS No:
C 910(526.8)
TAY

WHY DRAW A MAP?

Have you ever tried to tell friends how to get to your house? It's hard for them to remember where to turn left or right or go straight on. It's easier to draw them a map of the route to take.

As well as helping us find places or plan journeys, maps record information about things such as the weather, the number of people living in a place or the rocks under the ground. They can also show how an area has changed over time.

LATITUDE AND LONGITUDE
pages 30–31

GLOBES AND PROJECTIONS
pages 32–35

SYMBOLS AND SIGNS
pages 20–23

ferry
telephone
pylon
lighthouse
campsite
road
bridge
chapel
church
path

THE HIKER'S CODE

If you go on a hike in the countryside, take a detailed map and a compass (see page 26) to help you find the way. Plan your route first and don't try to walk too far.

- Always go walking with a friend or an adult.
- Tell someone where you are going and when you expect to get back.
- Wear stout shoes or boots and take food, drink and warm, waterproof clothes.
- Keep to the paths wherever possible.
- Take care not to leave litter, pick flowers, disturb animals or start fires.

WEATHER

Constellations

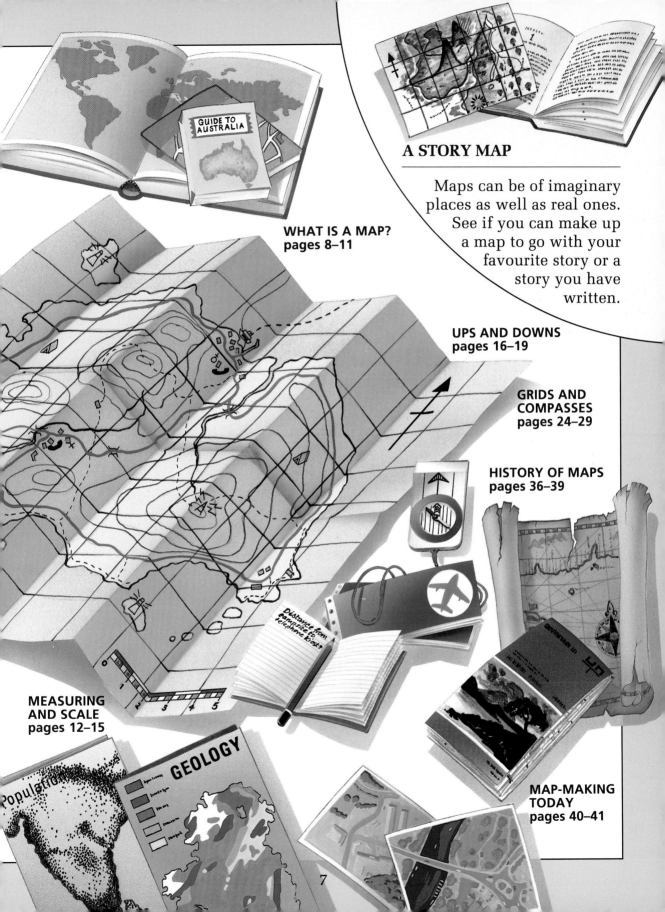

A STORY MAP

Maps can be of imaginary places as well as real ones. See if you can make up a map to go with your favourite story or a story you have written.

GUIDE TO AUSTRALIA

GEOLOGY

Population

Distance from campsite to telephone kiosk

WHAT IS A MAP?

A map is usually a flat picture of the world seen from above. It shows the sort of view you see looking down from a tall building or from an aeroplane.

Some maps are very accurate; others are just sketches of a place. Maps are drawn a lot smaller than the places they represent and they can't show every road, building or tree, or things that move about, such as cars or people. Map-makers have to choose the most important features to include.

ATLASES

An atlas is a book of maps. A world atlas contains maps of all the seven continents. The word atlas was first used by a 16th century map-maker, Mercator. He named his book of maps after the Greek god, Atlas, who was forced to carry the Earth on his head and shoulders as a punishment.

If you could fly above a maze, like a bird, you could see the way to the middle.

A map of a maze gives you a bird's eye view, so you can see at a glance the best route to take.

A map helps you to find your way through the maze of streets in a town, even if you've never been there before.

A BIRD'S EYE VIEW

Seen from above, familiar objects – such as bicycles or saucepans – look quite different. A round table just looks like a circle and could be a plate or a ball.

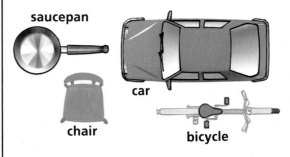

saucepan

car

chair

bicycle

Before you draw a map, practise drawing some objects from above.

1 Put some objects on a tray, with space between them.
2 Stand on a stool, look straight down, and sketch the outline shapes you see.

Show your friends your drawings and see if they can guess the objects.

COLLECTING MAPS

Maps are everywhere. See how many places you can spot them. You could make a scrapbook of some of the maps you collect, such as the ones on food labels, stamps, leaflets and postcards.

MY JOURNEY

Try drawing a sketch map of the journey from your house to a friend's house. Before you start, it may help to close your eyes and go over the route in your head. Can you see some other possible routes on this map?

DRAW A POSTER MAP

Travel agents use maps to show people where a holiday village is and what tourist attractions are nearby. Have a go at drawing a map for a poster advertising a place where you've been on holiday or somewhere you would like to go. Include things like the weather, restaurants, beaches, the wildlife, bus routes, airports, places to visit and so on.

You could make the map as a collage, using shells for the beaches, straws and ice-cream wafers to show refreshment areas, cloth for clothes shops, feathers for a bird reserve and leaves on cocktail sticks for trees in a forest.

DESIGN A MAZE

A maze is a series of narrow pathways through which you have to find your way to reach a particular point. There are usually dead ends to confuse you and make you go the wrong way. Look for examples of mazes in puzzle books or magazines.

You could draw your maze on squared paper, or base the design on a shape such as a circle, a tree or a zebra. Use thick, black lines to start with. How does the maze look different in colour? You can turn your maze into a treasure hunt with clues scattered throughout it. Or make a 3D maze.

MOVING FURNITURE

You can give your bedroom a whole new look by moving the furniture around. It's hard to imagine where the furniture will fit, but by drawing a map you can work this out without lifting a finger.

Here are three ways of arranging the same furniture.

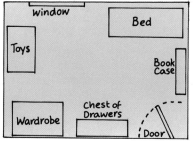

Can you think of others? These are sketches, but to draw an accurate map, you need to measure the size of the room and furniture first. Then you can draw a map to scale.

Turn over to find out more about scale.

11

MEASURING AND SCALE

When a map is drawn to scale, each detail is shown at the correct size compared to the other details. Everything is shrunk or scaled down by the same amount. So a street 5 m wide could be drawn 5 cm wide on a map and a wall 10 m long could be drawn 10 cm long.

Large-scale maps, such as road maps, show lots of detail. The larger the scale, the smaller the area shown. Small-scale maps show a large area with little detail. A map of the world is a very small-scale map.

MEASURING EQUIPMENT

Before maps can be drawn, surveyors have to measure angles and distances from certain key points to various features that will be included on the map. As well as tape measures, they use special electronic equipment, which measures distances using light or sound waves.

Try using the scale on a map to work out distances between places. Use a ruler for straight lines. Use string or the edge of a piece of paper for curved lines.

string

ruler

pencil

paper

The width of the duckpond is

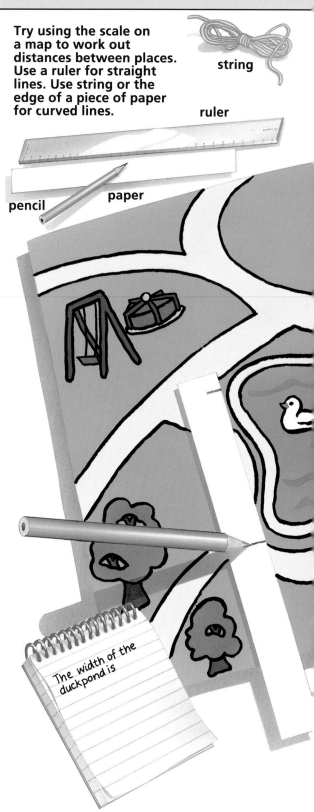

The scale can be shown as a line, or written in words or in a form such as 1:50,000. This means 1 unit on the map equals 50,000 units on the ground.

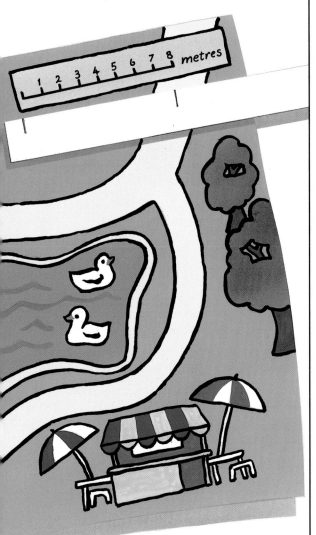

Mark the distance on the edge of a piece of paper. Then place the paper along the map scale to read off the actual distance on the ground.

BIGGER AND SMALLER

To help you understand map scales, try drawing your hand to a bigger or smaller scale. First draw round your hand on a large piece of squared paper. This gives a lifesize plan with a scale of 1:1.

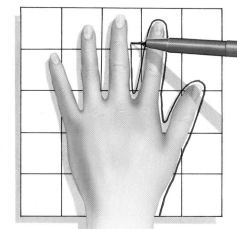

On a larger piece of paper, draw each square twice as big as the original ones. Then carefully copy, square by square, the outline of your hand on to the bigger squares. You will now have a map of your hand at a scale of 2:1.

Can you draw a hand map half the original size – a scale of 1:2? Or at a scale of 1:3?

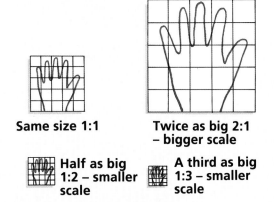

Same size 1:1

Twice as big 2:1 – bigger scale

Half as big 1:2 – smaller scale

A third as big 1:3 – smaller scale

MEASURING WITHOUT RULERS

Before rulers and tape measures were invented, people used parts of the body to help them measure things. The most important measure in ancient Egypt was the cubit – the distance from the elbow to the tip of the middle finger. The cubit was divided into seven smaller units, each measuring the width of a palm. In turn, a palm was made up of four digits (a digit was the width of the middle finger).

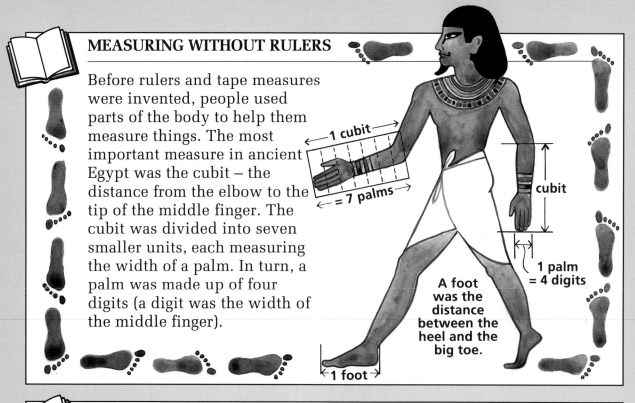

1 cubit

= 7 palms

cubit

1 palm = 4 digits

A foot was the distance between the heel and the big toe.

1 foot

HOW BIG?

The size of map scale people choose depends on how they will be using the map. If they want to find out about the whole of North America, they would need a small-scale map (say 1:35,000,000) which shows state boundaries, major cities, mountain ranges and so on. But if they want to find out about the city of New York, they need a larger scale map (say 1:30,000) which shows streets and buildings. A useful scale of map for exploring the countryside on foot is about 1:50,000.

A view as if you are standing next to a train in a station.

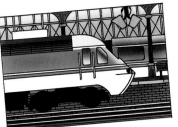

A view of the station placed in the town, to a smaller scale.

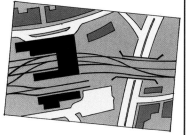

A bird's eye view of the same station to a large scale.

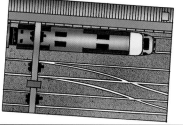

A view of the station, town and countryside round it, to a much smaller scale.

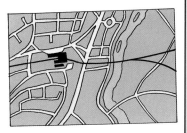

DECORATE A SCALE

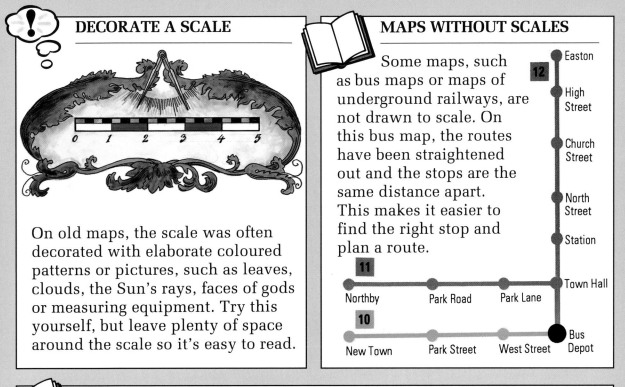

On old maps, the scale was often decorated with elaborate coloured patterns or pictures, such as leaves, clouds, the Sun's rays, faces of gods or measuring equipment. Try this yourself, but leave plenty of space around the scale so it's easy to read.

MAPS WITHOUT SCALES

Some maps, such as bus maps or maps of underground railways, are not drawn to scale. On this bus map, the routes have been straightened out and the stops are the same distance apart. This makes it easier to find the right stop and plan a route.

WHICH WAY TO THE FIRE?

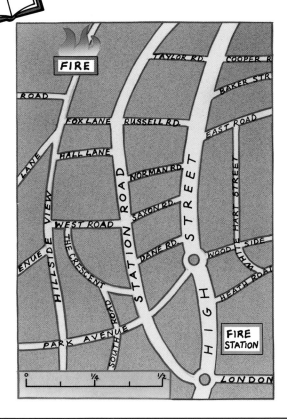

It is useful for emergency services, such as the fire service, to calculate distances from a map using the scale. Then they can send fire engines on the quickest route to a fire.

But they need to find out more from the map than just the distance. In these three possible routes, the shortest (1) is not the quickest, because traffic lights and narrow streets hold up the traffic.

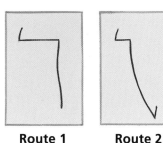

Route 1
2 km – 5 min

Route 2
2.5 km – 3 min

Route 3
3 km – 7 min

15

UPS AND DOWNS

Some maps show the shape or relief of the land – where it goes up and down, where there are hills, mountains, valleys, coasts and cliffs. These are called topographical maps. Land maps show heights and depths, measured above and below the average level of the sea, by pictures of hills, colours, shading or numbered lines called contours. Numbers giving the exact height at a particular point are called spot heights. Undersea maps, called charts, show the depths of the water measured when the water is at its lowest.

THE FIRST HILLS

Map-makers in the 16th and 17th centuries drew pictures of hillocks on maps to show relief. They shaded one side of each little hill with diagonal lines to make them look three-dimensional, but they did not use accurate heights or precise positions.

Hills and valleys can be shown by shading to look like the shadows cast by the Sun, or by hachures – little lines that follow the way the hills slope. Steeper slopes have darker lines.

Contour lines join up places that are the same height above sea level. They were not commonly used until the 19th century.

If colours are used to show height, the lowest land is usually yellow or green, higher land is brown and mountain tops are purple and white.

MAKE AN OLD MAP

Try making an old map to illustrate a story about a journey over a mountain range. Draw little pictures of the mountains in the style of the old map-makers.

This map goes with a story about King Ogel, imprisoned in Castle Dread by the evil Knight of Thoskor. The red line shows the way the King's army must go to reach him before the winter snows block the mountain passes . . . But you can make up your own storyline.

To make your map look old, stamp on it with muddy boots, spill tea on it, rub sand or soil over it, crumple it up or tear the edges.

Muddy boots

Spill tea

Rub in dirt

Tear the edges

Scrunch it up

DRAW CONTOURS

To see how contour lines work, build a mountain and make a contour map.

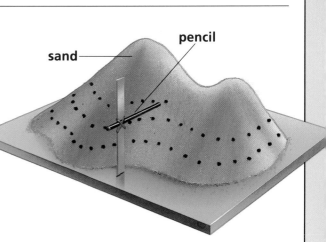

sand — pencil

1 Make the mountain out of damp sand or soil on a flat board. It's best to do this outside. With a pencil, make rows of holes all round the sand. Use a ruler to keep each row at the same height.

2 Join up the holes in each row by wrapping lengths of string around the mountain.

viewed from above

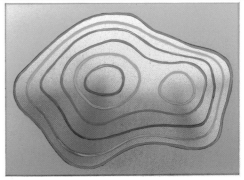

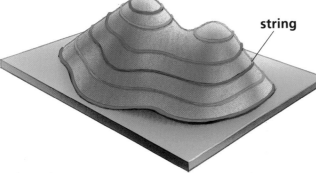

string

3 Now look down on the mountain and draw the string lines on paper. They should look like contour lines on a map. Are the lines closer together in some places? Is the slope gentle or steep there?

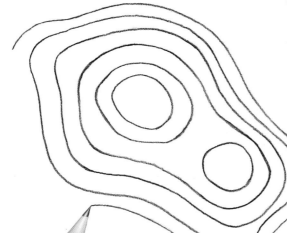

contour lines drawn on paper

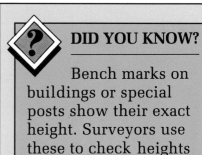

DID YOU KNOW?

Bench marks on buildings or special posts show their exact height. Surveyors use these to check heights in mapping work.

FACE CONTOURS

It's often hard to imagine the shape of the land by looking at a few contour lines on a map. It may help you to see a contour map of a familiar object, such as a face. The nose is like a hill with steep sides; the cheeks are wide, flat plains; the eye sockets are steep valley sides, and the forehead is a gentle slope.

A model of a face

A contour map of the same face

THE SHAPE OF THE LAND

Look out for contour lines like these on the maps you use. If the lines are close together, it means a steep slope. If they end suddenly at the coast, there are cliffs. A round contour shows the top of a hill.

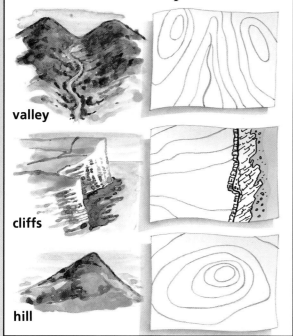

valley

cliffs

hill

UNDER THE SEA

To map the sea bed, surveyors measure the depth of the water using instruments called echo-sounders. They send down sound waves and record the time it takes for the echo to bounce back. We know how far sound travels in a certain time, so the surveyors use this to work out the depth of the water.

19

SYMBOLS AND SIGNS

To pack a lot of information into a small space, map-makers use symbols to stand for real features such as trees, railway stations or camp sites. Symbols bring a map to life; they can be useful even if they are quite small.

Some symbols do not look much like the features they represent. Other symbols do, such as those on tourist maps. The meanings of the symbols that are used on a map are explained in a key, which is sometimes called a legend.

AROUND THE WORLD

There is no international code for map symbols, so they vary in different countries. Here are some examples of symbols for the same features in Britain, France and the USA. In what ways are they different or similar?

	BRITAIN	USA	FRANCE
woodland			
motorways		69	
main roads			
tracks			
footpaths			
airports			

See if you can compare the keys on maps from several different countries.

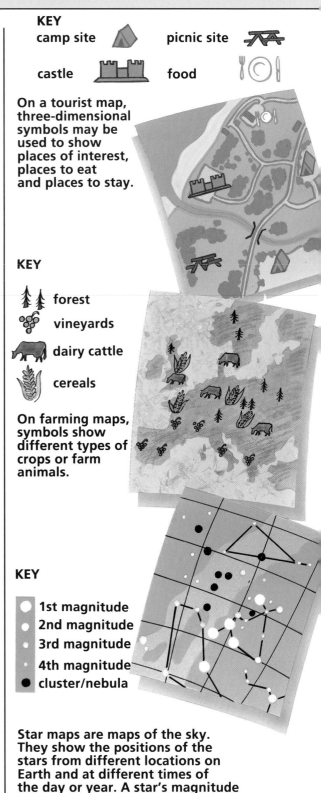

KEY

camp site   picnic site

castle   food

On a tourist map, three-dimensional symbols may be used to show places of interest, places to eat and places to stay.

KEY

forest

vineyards

dairy cattle

cereals

On farming maps, symbols show different types of crops or farm animals.

KEY

1st magnitude
2nd magnitude
3rd magnitude
4th magnitude
cluster/nebula

Star maps are maps of the sky. They show the positions of the stars from different locations on Earth and at different times of the day or year. A star's magnitude means its brightness.

clear   cloudy   overcast

rain ●   drizzle ◕   snow ✳

wind speed
and direction

10 knots

20 knots

30 knots

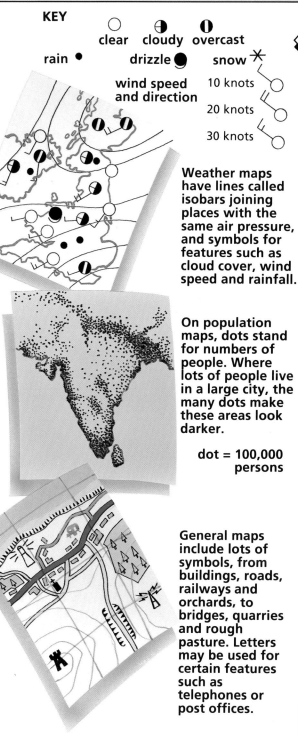

Weather maps have lines called isobars joining places with the same air pressure, and symbols for features such as cloud cover, wind speed and rainfall.

On population maps, dots stand for numbers of people. Where lots of people live in a large city, the many dots make these areas look darker.

dot = 100,000 persons

General maps include lots of symbols, from buildings, roads, railways and orchards, to bridges, quarries and rough pasture. Letters may be used for certain features such as telephones or post offices.

DESIGN YOUR OWN SYMBOLS

The main points about a map symbol are that it should be clear and easy to draw, and it must remind people immediately of the feature it represents. Symbols may look simple, but it takes a lot of thought to design them well. It's best to use as few lines as possible.

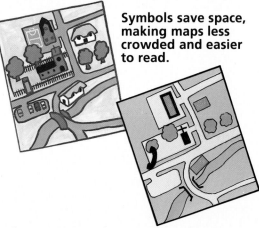

Symbols save space, making maps less crowded and easier to read.

Make a list of the symbols used for key features such as schools, hospitals, parks and post offices on a local map of your area. Then see if you can design your own versions. Which symbols would you use for a museum, a farm trail, a mosque or a theme park?

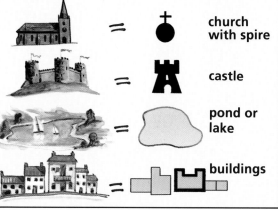

church
with spire

castle

pond or
lake

buildings

DRAW A TOURIST MAP

Tourist maps often have symbols which look like the real landmarks and are always large compared to the scale of the map.

See if you can draw a tourist map of your local area or a city you would like to visit. Include symbols for castles, museums, nature trails, swimming pools, boating lakes and so on. Keep the symbols large and lively so they look as if they are growing up from the surface of the map.

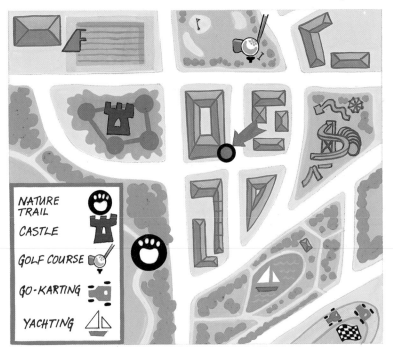

NATURE TRAIL

CASTLE

GOLF COURSE

GO-KARTING

YACHTING

INFORMATION MAPS

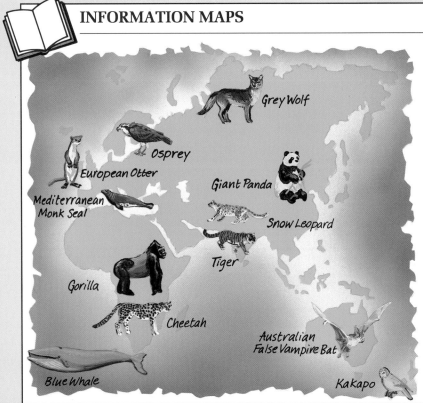

Grey Wolf

Osprey

European Otter

Mediterranean Monk Seal

Giant Panda

Snow Leopard

Tiger

Gorilla

Cheetah

Australian False Vampire Bat

Blue Whale

Kakapo

The symbols on a map are a good way of getting across information. For instance, a list of places where endangered animals live is hard to grasp. But a glance at symbols for the animals on a big map gives a much clearer picture and makes the information look more interesting.

On a small-scale map like this, you can only give a general idea of where each animal lives. On a large-scale map, the symbols can be located more accurately.

SYMBOLS AND SIGNS QUIZ

See if you can design your own symbols and challenge your friends to guess what they stand for. How many did they get right? How can you improve the symbols to make them clearer?

Can you guess what these symbols mean? The answers are upside down at the bottom of the page.

TIPS ON DRAWING SYMBOLS

• Don't draw too big – the symbols will be the size of peas on the map.
• Stick to simple, geometric shapes and bold, straight lines.
• Solid black shapes are clearer at a small size than coloured ones.
• Think about what a thing represents – the idea behind it – not what it actually looks like.
• Draw animals in characteristic poses, such as birds flying or monkeys swinging from branches.

SPACE BATTLE GAMES

You can use map symbols to plot movements. Try drawing a map of a battle in space between good and evil forces. You can base your map on a computer game if you like, or just use your imagination. Use symbols of different shapes and colours for the different armies.

You can either draw several maps of the battle at different stages, or cut out symbols for the space fighters from card and move them around on a base map. Looking at a map of the battle will help you plan your tactics.

Don't forget to include a key to go with your map.

Answers: a gifts, b electricity, c swimming pool, d no smoking, e tennis, f first aid, g refreshments, h crocodiles, i cycles, j telephone, k sunshine, l showers.

GRIDS AND COMPASSES

Many large-scale maps are covered with a network of lines dividing the map into equal-sized squares. This is called the map grid. Each grid line has a letter or a number, so we can find any point on the map by using the letters or numbers of the grid lines which cross at that point. This is called a grid reference.

Once we've found a place from its grid reference, we also need to know which direction to take in order to reach it. For this we use the north arrow printed on the map, together with a compass.

SEA CHARTS

Over 500 years ago, the Marshall Islanders of the Pacific Ocean planned their journeys using maps made out of sticks and shells. Shells marked the position of islands on a network of sticks, rather like a grid. Curved sticks represented the pattern of ocean currents.

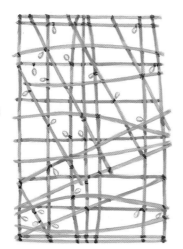

On a map without grid lines, it's hard to describe the exact position of a place. How would you tell people where the treasure is buried on this map?

When the map has a grid over the top, it's easy to find the treasure. Follow line D up and line 3 across – the treasure is where the lines cross, at D3.

Some grids use numbers to label all the lines. Others have letters going one way and numbers the other.

DRAW A GRID

To show a friend exactly where to meet you, draw a map with grid lines on top and give a grid reference of the meeting place. You could draw the map on squared paper and then rule over some lines in ink to make big squares. Or measure your own network of squares with a ruler.

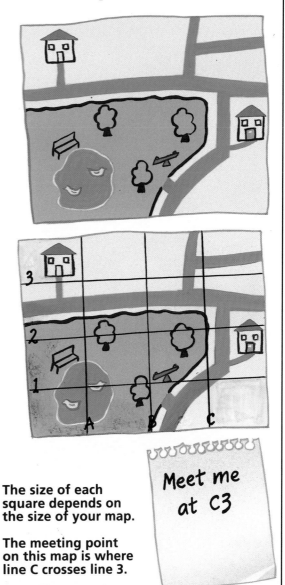

The size of each square depends on the size of your map.

The meeting point on this map is where line C crosses line 3.

Meet me at C3

USING A GRID

The grid reference for a whole square is for the grid lines that cross in the bottom left-hand corner of the square – such as 63 in the picture on the right.

First read the numbers at the top or bottom of the map. They are called eastings, because their numbers increase eastwards. Then read the numbers at the sides. They are called northings, as their numbers increase northwards.

For a more accurate reference, you need to imagine each square is divided into 10. Add a number between 0 and 9 to each grid line number. This gives a reference such as 7545 in this picture.

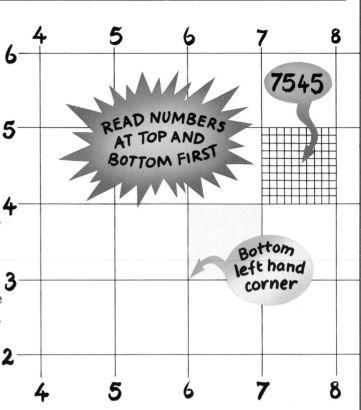

READ NUMBERS AT TOP AND BOTTOM FIRST

7545

Bottom left hand corner

HOW TO USE A COMPASS

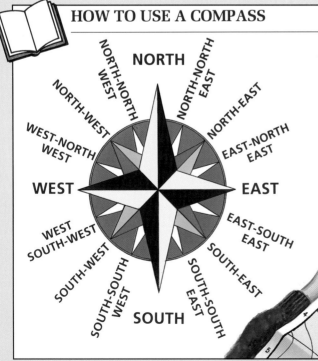

NORTH
NORTH-NORTH WEST
NORTH-NORTH EAST
NORTH-WEST
NORTH-EAST
WEST-NORTH WEST
EAST-NORTH EAST
WEST
EAST
WEST SOUTH-WEST
EAST-SOUTH EAST
SOUTH-WEST
SOUTH-EAST
SOUTH-SOUTH WEST
SOUTH-SOUTH EAST
SOUTH

A compass needle is a magnet, which always points to the Earth's magnetic poles. To work out which way to go, place a compass on the map and turn the map around until the north arrow on the map points in the same direction as the compass needle. A compass helps you find the way even in fog when you can't see where you are going.

MAKE A COMPASS

WHAT YOU NEED

needle

magnet

slice of cork

saucer of water

How to make it

1 To turn the needle into a magnet, stroke the magnet along the needle about 50 times. Stroke the magnet in one direction only.

2 Float the cork on the saucer of water and balance the needle on the cork.

3 The needle will swing round to point north-south. Check the direction with a real compass. Label north and south on the saucer's edge.

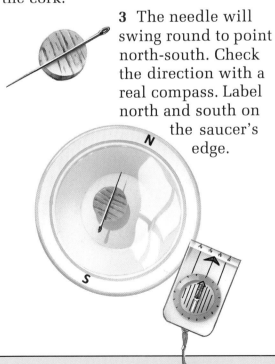

WHY COMPASSES WORK

A compass needle points north-south because it is a tiny magnet being pulled by magnetic forces deep inside the Earth. The Earth itself is like a gigantic magnet with a magnetic north and a magnetic south pole. The south pole of the needle is pulled towards the North Pole of the Earth, and vice versa, because opposite poles attract each other.

DID YOU KNOW?

There are three types of north. True north is at the North Pole. Grid north, where the grid lines on a map lead to, is a different point. Magnetic north is near the North Pole, about 1,600 km away. Magnetic north moves about, whereas the directions of true north and grid north never change year by year. Look out for the different north arrows on the edge of local large-scale maps.

STAR MAPS

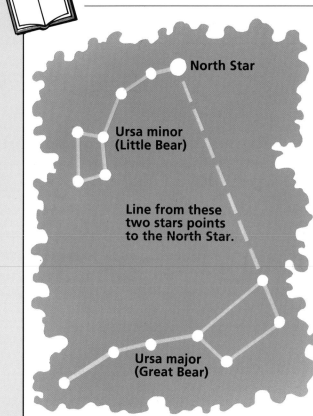

North Star

Ursa minor
(Little Bear)

Line from these
two stars points
to the North Star.

Ursa major
(Great Bear)

For thousands of years, navigators have used the positions of the stars to find their way across seas and oceans at night. The stars are grouped in constellations which form different patterns, like maps in the sky.

One of the most important stars for finding directions in the northern hemisphere is the North Star. This is above the North Pole and stays more or less in the same place. The North Star is the brightest star in the constellation of the Little Bear.

If you find the nearby constellation of the Great Bear (which looks like a saucepan) and follow a line upwards from the two stars at the front of the pan, you will come to the North Star.

COMPASS ROSES

fleur-de-lys

Map-makers used to decorate compass points on maps quite elaborately. These were called compass roses because they looked like petals. Sometimes there was a special symbol for north, such as the fleur-de-lys.

ORIENTEERING

Orienteering is the sport of finding your way around the countryside using a map and a compass. Competitors have to find a number of points from grid references and written descriptions. The winner is the one who completes the course in the shortest time.

TREASURE HUNT GAME

Draw and label a grid of squares on thick card. In some of the squares, write instructions to make the players go backwards or forwards a few squares. Some instructions should be grid references and some compass directions.

The first player to reach the treasure wins the game.

Use buttons as counters, throw a six to start and then throw the dice again to see how many squares to move your button.

LATITUDE AND LONGITUDE

On globes and maps of large areas of the world, a grid of imaginary lines called latitude and longitude help us to find places. Lines of longitude (or meridians) go up and down a map and lines of latitude (or parallels) go across.

Lines of longitude are measured in degrees east or west of a line drawn from the North Pole, through Greenwich in London, England, to the South Pole. Lines of latitude are measured in degrees north or south of the equator, an imaginary line around the middle of the Earth.

GREENWICH MERIDIAN

The 0° line of longitude is marked on the ground at Greenwich in London. It is called the Greenwich Meridian or the Great Meridian. Every place in the world that lies north or south along this line has the same time, called Greenwich Mean Time, or GMT for short.

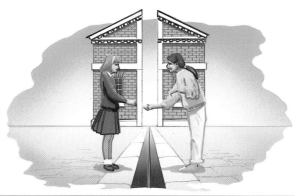

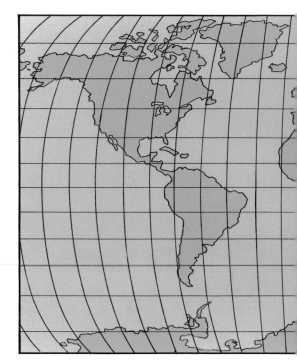

This map shows the lines of latitude and longitude.

North Pole

Greenwi⟨

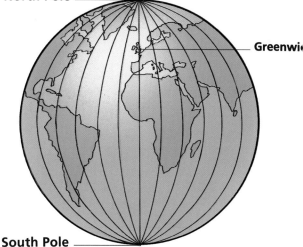

South Pole

Lines of longitude are wide apart at the equator and closer together at the poles. Greenwich is 0° longitude. There are 180 degrees of longitude west of Greenwich and 180 degrees east of Greenwich.

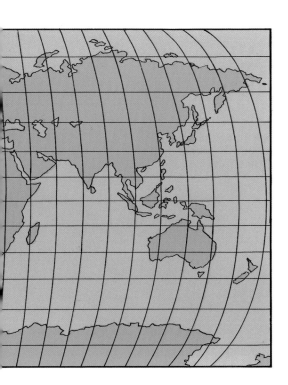

FINDING PLACES

You can find any place from a reference to the lines of latitude and longitude at that point. Latitude is given first. For instance, New York in the USA is located at the point where the 41° North line of latitude crosses the 74° West line of longitude – 41° N, 74° W.

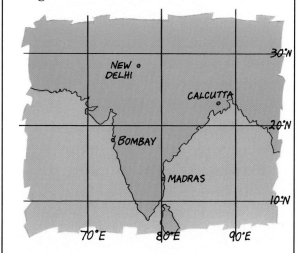

Can you work out references for the cities on the map above?

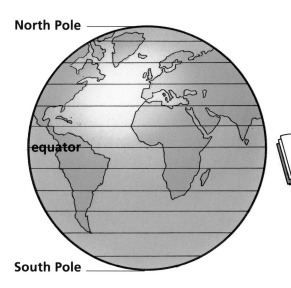

North Pole

equator

South Pole

The equator is 0° latitude. There are 90 degrees of latitude north of it and 90 degrees south of it. The latitude of the North Pole is 90° north and the latitude of the South Pole is 90° south.

TIME ZONES

Time across the world is worked out from the 0° line of longitude at Greenwich. As the Earth turns through 15° of longitude each hour, the time changes by 1 hour every 15° east or west of Greenwich. This divides the world into 24 time zones, each with a difference of 1 hour. East of Greenwich, the time is ahead; to the west, the time is behind.

GLOBES AND PROJECTIONS

The Earth is round, so the only accurate map of the Earth is a globe. But globes are expensive to make and hard to carry around in your pocket. So map-makers transfer, or project, the curved surface of the world on to flat sheets of paper. There are over 200 ways of doing this, but they all involve stretching or shrinking part of the globe.

Some projections distort size and distance; others show size or distance well but distort shapes. All map projections use lines of latitude and longitude to locate places in the right spot.

THE FIRST GLOBES

The ancient Greeks were the first to work out that the Earth is round. In 100 BC Crates tried to show the continents in their proper positions by plotting them on a globe. But the world he knew of covered just a quarter of the estimated size of the globe. So he added three imaginary continents to make it neat and balanced.

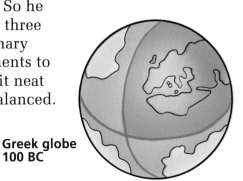

Greek globe 100 BC

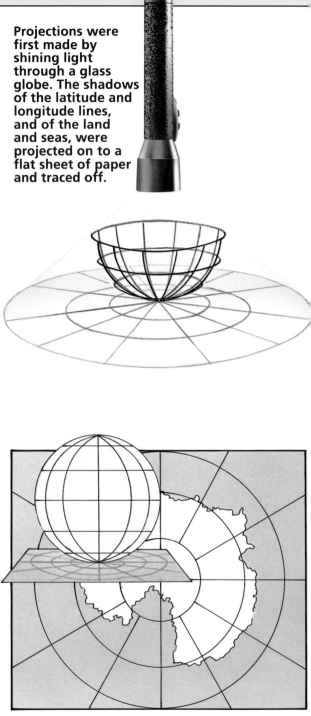

Projections were first made by shining light through a glass globe. The shadows of the latitude and longitude lines, and of the land and seas, were projected on to a flat sheet of paper and traced off.

An azimuthal projection is made as if one point on the globe (the centre or "azimuth") is touching a flat plane. It is circular, but can show only half the world at a time. It shows true directions from one point on the map to another, but is distorted away from the centre.

A conical projection is made as if a cone is placed over the globe and then spread out in a flat fan shape. Latitude lines look curved. The conical projection shows areas, distances and directions fairly accurately. Distortions increase away from the line where the cone touches the globe.

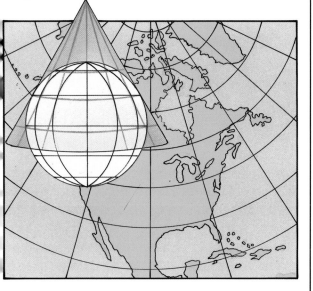

A cylindrical projection is made as if a cylinder is wrapped around the globe and then rolled flat. Longitude lines run straight, at right angles to latitude lines. The projection can show almost the whole world, but it makes countries near the Poles too large.

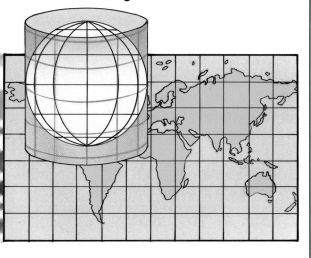

ROUND EARTH, FLAT MAPS

Find out for yourself how difficult it is to transfer the round Earth on to a flat piece of paper. First draw a rough map of the world on to an orange.

Then peel the orange, keeping the peel in one piece if you can. Now try to lay the peel out flat. What happens to the shapes of the continents? How is your orange-peel map different from the world maps in atlases?

Have you ever struggled to wrap up a round object, such as a soccer ball, in a flat piece of paper? It's almost impossible! There's lots of spare paper and it's hard to fold it neatly and tape it together.

MAKING GLOBE MAPS

On a globe, the continents are the right size and shape and all are in the right position in relation to the others. In the 15th century, many globes were made by drawing a map of the world on to long strips of paper with pointed ends.

The strips were then carefully pasted on to a hollow wooden ball so they fitted perfectly together. Globes could be made from different numbers of strips, but they had to be drawn very accurately. Some globes are still made in this way today.

INTERRUPTED PROJECTIONS

Some map-makers try to keep the right shapes and spacing of the continents and cut up the map. This produces an interrupted projection, like this one, which is more of a diagram than a map because of all the gaps.

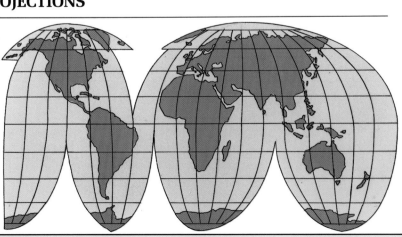

MERCATOR'S PROJECTION

In 1569, Mercator found a way of showing the world on a flat map. He took a globe map and stretched the lands north and south of the equator to fill in the gaps on the flat map. The projection allowed sailors to plot a straight line

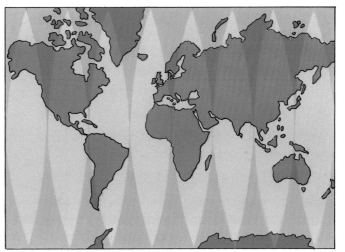

The dark grey areas have been stretched.

between two points accurately. But the scale is different from one part of the map to another, and countries near the Poles are far too big.

GLOBES AND ATLASES

To see how different projections change the size and shape of different countries and continents, look in an atlas and carry out a survey. How many different projections can you find? They are often named after the people who invented them, such as

Mercator, Peters or Robinson.

Also compare the same countries or continents on a globe and in an atlas. How different are the sizes? Which projections are most accurate? Countries furthest from the equator, such as Greenland, are often the most distorted.

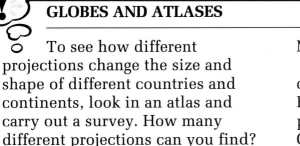

Mexico

Greenland

Mexico and Greenland are really almost the same size, as you can see on a globe.

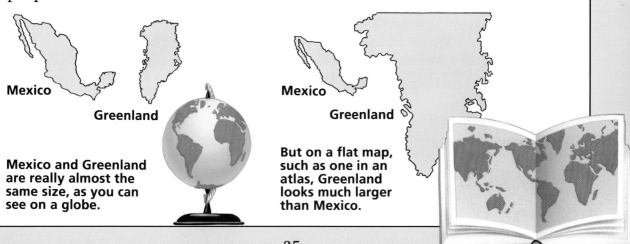

Mexico

Greenland

But on a flat map, such as one in an atlas, Greenland looks much larger than Mexico.

HISTORY OF MAPS

People have used sketch maps, often just scratched in the ground, for thousands of years. The first attempt at a flat map of the whole world was made by Marinus of Tyre and completed by Ptolemy in AD 160. His maps were copied until the Middle Ages. Many medieval maps showed a view of the world according to religious teachings, not what the world was actually like. Nowadays, we can use aerial photographs, satellite photographs and computers to make very accurate and detailed maps of the world.

EXPLORING THE WORLD

In the Middle Ages, most people thought the world was flat and that you would fall off the edge if you sailed too far out to sea. Explorers such as Christopher Columbus and Ferdinand Magellan changed these ideas. In 1519 Magellan led the first round-the-world voyage and collected valuable information for European map-makers about countries outside Europe.

The oldest known map was scratched on a clay tablet in about 2300 BC. It marks the boundaries of fields, a river, and mountains drawn in a pattern like fish scales.

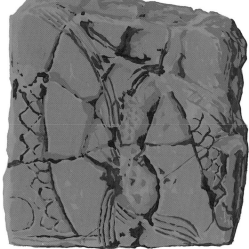

Ptolemy, a Greek astronomer and geographer, was the first great map-maker. He drew maps to different scales and suggested that maps show information such as climate and population density as well as landscape features.

Medieval maps like this Hereford world map were based on writings in the Bible and put Jerusalem at the centre of the world. They were called T-in-O maps because of their shape.

the Orient (East)

Jerusalem

Europe   Africa

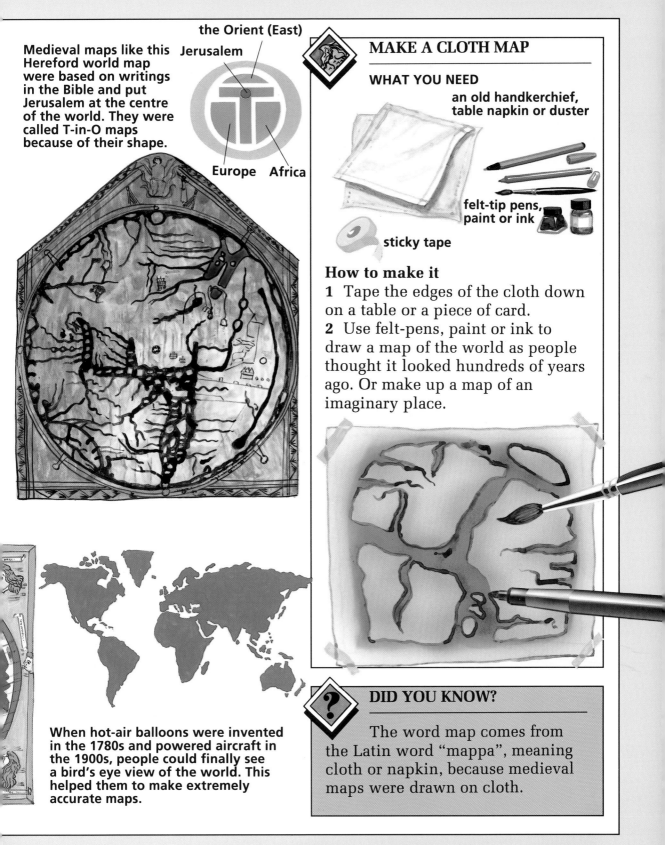

When hot-air balloons were invented in the 1780s and powered aircraft in the 1900s, people could finally see a bird's eye view of the world. This helped them to make extremely accurate maps.

MAKE A CLOTH MAP

WHAT YOU NEED

an old handkerchief, table napkin or duster

felt-tip pens, paint or ink

sticky tape

How to make it

1 Tape the edges of the cloth down on a table or a piece of card.
2 Use felt-pens, paint or ink to draw a map of the world as people thought it looked hundreds of years ago. Or make up a map of an imaginary place.

DID YOU KNOW?

The word map comes from the Latin word "mappa", meaning cloth or napkin, because medieval maps were drawn on cloth.

DECORATE A MAP

Early maps were works of art, drawn or painted by hand. When the map-makers came to areas they knew little about, or to large areas of sea, they filled these in with pictures of things such as cherubs, coats of arms, sea monsters, mermaids, flags and old sailing ships. Use your imagination and see if you can decorate an old map in this kind of style.

MAP SHAPES

Many old maps were drawn in the shape of animals or people – some as a form of decoration, some as a joke. Have a look in an atlas and see if the shapes of any countries remind you of anything. Or make up an imaginary island map in the shape of an animal.

The black and white markings on a fresian cow can be turned into a map of the world.

A map of Great Britain can be turned into a robber running.

A map of Italy can become a boot.

38

STRIP OR LINEAR MAPS

Early coaching maps were narrow vertical strips showing the route as a straight line – like bus maps today (see page 15). Travellers read the maps from bottom to top. A compass and north arrow showed the direction on each strip.

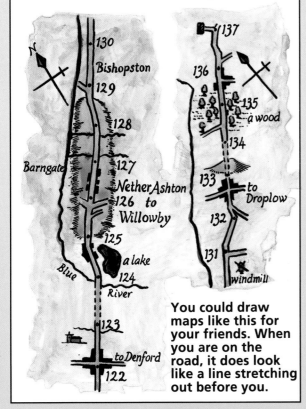

You could draw maps like this for your friends. When you are on the road, it does look like a line stretching out before you.

CARVED MAPS

The Inuit of Greenland and Canada used to carve very accurate maps out of driftwood. The curves of the wood represented the shape of the coastline and showed where bays and rivers were. This was important both for the Inuit's fishing industry and for their survival.

MODEL A MAP

See if you can make a model of a real stretch of coastline or an island out of modelling clay. Choose a place in an atlas and shape the clay with your fingers and an old spoon. When you have finished, leave the clay to set hard.

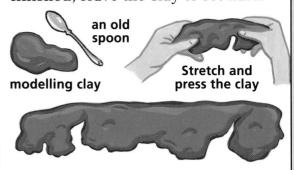

an old spoon

modelling clay

Stretch and press the clay

DID YOU KNOW?

In the 13th century, Mediterranean traders used charts drawn on parchment to help them find harbours along the coasts. The charts were known as portolan charts because they were portable and could be carried around instead of being kept in libraries. They were used until the 1600s.

MAP-MAKING TODAY

Three main groups of people work to produce a map: surveyors measure and record the positions of things and the shape of the Earth's surface; cartographers design and draw the map; and printers reproduce the drawing in colour and make copies.

Nowadays, aerial photographs, satellite photographs and computers help us to draw maps more quickly and accurately than ever before. Before aerial photographs are taken, surveyors measure the position and heights of a network of points on the ground and mark them so they will show up on the photographs.

PICTURES FROM SPACE

Satellites and manned spaceships orbiting the Earth send back detailed pictures of the Earth. The quality of the satellite images is improving all the time, but there will always be a need for surveyors to take measurements on the ground.

Aerial photographs are taken with a special camera fitted into the floor of an aircraft. They usually show a view of the land looking directly downwards. The plane flies along a carefully planned flight path and the camera takes photographs automatically at regular intervals.

If map-makers look at two overlapping aerial photographs through a stereoscope, they see the land in three dimensions. Stereo plotting machines show a 3D view of the ground and can be used to draw contours, relief and landscape features.

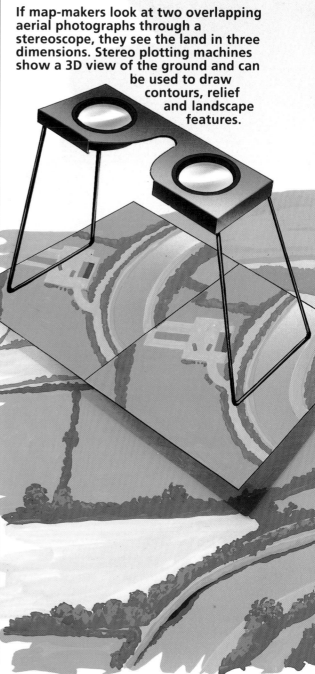

COMPUTER MAPS

Computers can be used to draw maps much faster than people can do by hand. Special instruments scan a photograph and turn it into a series of coded numbers. Then an automatic plotting machine linked to the computer uses the numbers to draw lines or patterns at any scale that is chosen.

TALKING MAPS IN CARS

Maps coded on to compact disc can be displayed on a screen in cars. The driver types in a code for the journey and the computer selects the shortest route, avoiding traffic jams and roadworks.

A plane taking aerial photographs flies at a constant height and takes a series of overlapping photographs. Every point on the ground is covered by at least two photographs, so no detail is lost.

USEFUL ADDRESSES AND FURTHER INFORMATION

Geographical organizations

Geographical Association,
343 Fulwood Road, Sheffield
S10 3BP.

Ordnance Survey,
Romsey Road, Maybush,
Southampton SO9 4DH.

National Geographic Society,
17th & M Streets, Washington,
D.C. 20036.
Membership in Britain:
Freepost, PO Box 19, Guildford,
Surrey GU3 3BR.

Map shops

Stanfords,
12–14 Long Acre, London WC2E 9LP.
(Wide selection of all types of maps,
geographical and travel books, atlases
and globes.)

The Map Store Inc.,
1636 Eye Street NW, Washington,
D.C. 20006.
(Map projections, atlases, globes and
objects decorated with maps.
Has mail order catalogue.)

Rand McNally,
PO Box 7600, Chicago, Illinois 60680.
(Atlases and all types of maps.
Stores in New York, Chicago and
San Francisco.)

Wall charts

Collins-Longman Atlases,
Freepost, Burnt Mill, Harlow,
Essex CM20 2YD.
(*Mapskills World Wallmap*; *Mapskills
Wallmap set 1: Relief Features*;
Mapskills Wallmap set 2: Countries.)

Pictorial Charts Educational Trust,
27 Kirchen Road, London W13 OUD.
(*What is a Map?*, *Mapping the Hills*,
Map and Scale, *Mapping Space*,
Mapping the Street, *The Built
Environment*, *Mapping the Weather*,
Maps and Direction, *Signs and
Symbols.*)

Packs

Meteorological Office,
Public Services, London Road,
Bracknell, Berkshire RG12 2SZ.
(General information pack on weather
and weather forecasting.)

Some helpful books

Look in your local library, your
school library or local bookshops.

**Maps and Mazes: A First Guide to
Map Making**
Gillian Chapman and Pam Robson,
Simon & Schuster Young Books.

Maps and Mapping
Barbara Taylor, Kingfisher Books.

Maps and Map-making
(Young Explorer series)
Mark C.W. Sleep, Wayland.

Maps and Globes
(Topics series)
David Lambert, Wayland.

Measuring and Maps
(Hands on Geography series)
Keith Lye, Franklin Watts.

Maps and Journeys: Our Globe, Our World
(Roundabouts series)
Kate Petty, A & C Black.

Bright Ideas: Geography
Merryn Hutchings and Alistair Ross,
Scholastic Publications Ltd.

Make It Work! Earth
Wendy Baker and Andrew Haslam,
Two-can Publishing.

On the Map
David Boardman, BBC Books.

Finding the Way
(Moving Around the World series)
Michael Pollard, Macmillan.

How the Earth Works
(Eyewitness Science Guides)
John Farndon, Dorling Kindersley.

Basic Geography for Tourism and Leisure
Gill Rollins, Macmillan Education Ltd.

Your Book of Maps and Map Reading
R. B. Matkin, Faber & Faber.

Let's Look at Maps & Mapmaking
Rowland W. Purton, Frederick Muller.

Maps and How to Read Them
Philip A. Sauvain, Franklin Watts.

Measuring and Computing
(Cambridge Science Universe series)
Cambridge University Press.

Time and Clocks
(Wake up to the World of Science series)
Kay Davies and Wendy Oldfield,
Burke Publishing Company Limited.

Mapwork 1
David Flint and Mandy Suhr and
Mapwork 2
Julie Warne and Mandy Suhr, Wayland

Atlases

The Picture Atlas of the World
Richard Kemp and Brian Delf, Dorling Kindersley.

Atlas
(Picture Pocket series)
Lionel Bender, Kingfisher Books.

Kingfisher Children's World Atlas
Kingfisher.

Wayland Atlas for the World
Wayland.

Oxford Rainbow Atlas
Patrick Wiegand, Oxford University Press.

GLOSSARY

Aerial photograph a photograph taken from an aircraft, usually from a fixed point looking straight down on the land below.

Altitude the height of a place above sea level.

Atlas a book of maps.

Cartographer a person who draws maps.

Chart a map used to navigate by sea or by air.

Climate map one which shows the usual pattern of the weather over the whole world or part of the world.

Compass an instrument for finding your way, with a needle that points to magnetic north or true north.

Contour a line on a map which joins points that are the same height above sea level.

Co-ordinates two sets of letters or numbers that refer to a particular point on a map grid.

Cubit an ancient unit of measurement – the length of the arm from the elbow to the middle fingertip.

Eastings the grid lines going vertically up and down a map. Eastings always come before northings in a grid reference.

Equator an imaginary line dividing the Earth into two equal halves. It is the line of 0° latitude and is more than 38,600 km long.

Globe a sphere which shows the true position and shape of the land, seas and oceans of the world.

Graticule a network of latitude and longitude lines on a map or a globe.

Greenwich Mean Time (GMT) the time at Greenwich, London, used as the basis to work out the time zones all over the world. If you travel west of Greenwich, you need to put your watch back one hour for every time zone you cross. If you travel east, you put your watch forward one hour for each zone.

Grid a framework of squares on a map which helps to locate points easily and accurately. Different countries use slightly different types of grid. Instructions on how to use the grid are usually printed on the edge of the map.

Grid reference the code of numbers or letters and numbers which describes the position of a point on a map.

International Date Line an imaginary line 180° longitude west or east of Greenwich. There is 24 hours difference on either side of the date line. If you cross it travelling eastwards, you go back 24 hours. If you cross it travelling westwards, you go forward 24 hours.

Key a list explaining the symbols and codes on a map. It is sometimes called a legend.

Latitude imaginary lines parallel to the equator, which run horizontally around the world. They are used to locate points north and south of the equator and are sometimes called parallels.

Longitude imaginary lines (also called meridians) which run at right angles to the equator and meet at the North and South Poles. They are used to locate points east and west of the Prime Meridian, which passes through Greenwich, London.

Northings the grid lines going horizontally across a map. They come after eastings in a grid reference.

Ordnance Survey detailed maps of Great Britain, first produced about 200 years ago to help the army move about the countryside more efficiently. (The word "ordnance" is used for anything to do with the military.) The first Ordnance Survey map was of Kent and it was produced in 1801.

Orienteering the competitive sport of finding your way across rough countryside using a map and a compass.

Political map one which shows the location and boundaries of countries, towns and cities.

Population map one which shows where numbers of people live and where cities are.

Prime Meridian the line of 0° longitude, which passes from the North Pole, through Greenwich, in London in England, to the South Pole.

Projection a representation of the curved surface of the Earth on a flat surface. A projection can show the correct scale, the correct area or the correct direction, but never all three at the same time. The first projection was produced by a Dutch map-maker, Mercator, in 1569.

Relief differences in the height of the land.

Relief map one which shows the location and shape of physical features, such as mountains, rivers, valleys, lakes and seas.

Satellite an artifical body placed in orbit around the Earth or another planet. Photographs of Earth taken from satellites have helped map-makers to produce very accurate maps.

Scale the number of units of measurement on the ground represented by one unit on a map. Large-scale maps cover a small area of country in detail. Small-scale maps cover large areas of country – even the whole world.

Sea level the average level, or "height", of the surface of the sea between high and low tide.

Spot height the exact height of a particular point marked on a map.

Symbol on a map, something that stands as a sign to represent a real feature.

INDEX